For little brown girls everywhere who have never seen themselves in love.

With love,
Keea Taylor

I Still Do

*A Celebration of
African-American Weddings*

by

Kea Taylor

For my husband, Rob
who has loved me fearlessly and courageously
and by doing so, has taught me to do the same.

For our boys Mike, Rob and Rell -
who will make great husbands one day.

And for my parents Sam and Cynthia Prather-
thank you for always choosing love.

It's because of you
that I still do.

Published by:
Imagine Photography
3717 Georgia Ave., NW
Washington, DC 20010

Copyright 2009 Kea Taylor

All rights reserved under International and Pan-American Copyright Conventions. No part of this book may be reproduced, stored in a retrieval system, or transmitted in any form, or by any means, electronic, mechanical, photocopyng, recording or otherwise without prior written permission of the copyright owner.

For information see:
 www.istilldoweddings.com

Cover and Title Page Photography: Kea Taylor (top right photo of groomsmen laughing by Chris Thomas for Imagine Photography)
Historic Cover Photos: Photographers unknown. Family photographs of author's parents' and grandparents' weddings courtesy of Cynthia Prather
Edited by Cynthia Prather and Edith Hancock
Book Design and Layout: Kea Taylor
Printed in the United States of America

2010
First Edition

ISBN 0615313205
ISBN 978-0-615-31320-7

LCCN 2009912504

I Still Do

Table of Contents

INTRODUCTION	6
IN THE BEGINNING...(ENGAGEMENT PORTRAITS)	9
EVERY THING BEAUTIFUL...(GETTING READY)	21
A SEAL UPON THINE HEART...(CEREMONIES)	45
BETTER THAN WINE...(POSED PORTRAITS)	69
A TIME TO DANCE...(THE RECEPTION)	87
AND THEY SHALL BE ONE...(DEPARTURES)	109
IT SHALL BE FOREVER...(FINAL THOUGHTS)	115
DETAILS...(APPENDIX)	
GLOSSARY OF AFRICAN TERMS AND SYMBOLS	118
DECORATION IDEAS	120
FINAL THOUGHTS	122
PHOTO CREDITS	124

INTRODUCTION

"PEOPLE ARE STILL GETTING MARRIED THESE DAYS?"

It could have been any one of the nights that I ventured out on the social scene filled with beautiful, well-dressed and polished, chocolate 30-somethings. In Washington, DC--a city wrought with well-educated power players and "inside trackers," it was (and still is) quite common to be asked by a total stranger, "So what do you do?" I had no problem telling people what I do, but I was often amused by the response. A typical conversation would go like this:

Me. "I'm a photographer."

Them. "Really? That's all you do? Take pictures?" *(Silence)* "What do you take pictures of? I mean do you work for a newspaper or something?"

Me. "No, I work for myself...but I shoot mostly people, buildings, events...and lots of weddings."

Them. (Look of mock horror and shock) "People are still getting married these days?"

Me. (With a shrug of the shoulders and a half nod and same mock enthusiasm) "Yep."

"IT WAS AS THOUGH THE AGE-OLD RITE OF PASSAGE -- GETTING MARRIED HAD GONE THE WAY OF PARACHUTE PANTS AND BELL BOTTOMS...IT JUST WENT OUT OF STYLE."

It was as though the age-old rite of passage/foundation of civilization of getting married had gone the way of parachute pants and bell bottoms...it just went out of style.

Then came Barack and Michelle. And all of the sudden, there were these images that it was as if our generation had never seen before. A strikingly beautiful Black man and woman actually in love? Not complaining about one another or professing the joys of swinging? We ate it up and responded as though they were authentic pioneers. Images of the happy Obamas flew off the shelves and flooded inboxes. In this age of depressing divorce statistics, down-low brothers and trashy reality TV, we were starved for confirmation that true love between Black men and women still exists--*somewhere*. Just their image alone quenched our unconscious thirst and made us feel, well...better.

I was both curious and amazed by the transformative power of this happy couple. Feeling at times like a kill-joy, I would ask whenever I could, "But what's so special about them?" In beauty salons and grocery stores everywhere, people would exclaim, "They look so happy! You can tell they're really in love...and Michelle's a *real* Black woman." Okay but even that didn't fully explain such obsession to me. I mean, "real" Black people have been in love for years...any one of us can name a grandparent, neighbor or church member that's been married 50 years. Why such obsession with images of the first couple? The general response basically boiled down to, "We know it exists. It's just so nice to actually see it."

"WE KNOW IT EXISTS. IT'S JUST SO NICE TO ACTUALLY SEE IT."

Then it hit me. ("Aha" as Oprah would say).

My experience seeing Black people in love was *not* the norm. I took for granted the newly-engaged brides and grooms that wistfully tell me about their engagements and dreams for their wedding day. I'd taken for granted the hundreds of first kisses, proud parents' toasts and infinite other touching moments that have resulted in thousands of images of beautiful sepia couples that now fill my studio. And if photos of just *one* couple had the power to stir so many, how many people would be encouraged by the thousands of images that now sit filed away in albums (or even worse, on my backup drives)?

So I decided to share.

"THE PAGES OF THIS BOOK ARE NOT FILLED WITH GRANDIOSE CEREMONIES."

I must warn you. Unlike the bridal magazines, I am not selling products or the idea of idyllic romance. The pages of this book are not just filled with grandiose ceremonies designed to fill young womens' heads with dreams of expensive fairy-tale weddings. I love a good Preston Bailey wedding as much as the next girl, but just as love takes many shapes and forms...so do wedding celebrations. These pages are simply my favorite images from the ceremonies I've had the pleasure of photographing over the past ten years. They range from people being intimately married in their uncle's living room to ocean-front weddings in Jamaica and Puerto Rico. I tell my clients often, if you can afford a large wedding...go for it. If not, keep it simple. It can still be beautiful and you'll be married at the end of the day just the same. As long as the priority remains to aspire to love, all weddings are equally memorable (and photogenic).

To add to the pretty pictures, I've also included stories from some of my favorite newly-married couples who have generously shared the personal struggles they've encountered while working to build their own successful marriages in this new millennium. While each of their stories is uniquely inspiring, there is a common theme. It is an amazing blessing to find a partner to share life with, but choosing to marry is accepting a calling to make an adult, lifelong commitment to invest time, energy, resources, and love in yourself and another person and even your community-- forever. And it's not always romantic.

Some questioned why I would incorporate such "unromantic" stories into such a lovely collection of pictures. In response, I can just hear the wise philosopher and singer Frankie Beverly profoundly serenading us, "Joy and pain, are like sunshine and rain...where there's a flower, there's the sun and the rain...it's wonderful, they're both one in the same." I cannot tell you how often I talk with clients (who often become friends after the wedding) that just want/need to be reassured that the occasional conflict is okay. And it is. Our conversations have been a gift and taught me some fundamental truths that have been on my heart to share. We all have problems, we all have the capacity to overcome them but only true *love* gives us the grace to be beautiful and inspire others in the process.

"EVEN IF YOU'RE NOT MARRYING THE FUTURE PRESIDENT, IMAGES OF THE COUPLES ON THESE PAGES ARE EQUALLY INSPIRING... IF NOT MORE...BECAUSE THESE ARE EVERYDAY PEOPLE."

As Barack and Michelle have revealed, images of genuine love possess a distinct transformative, uplifting, reassuring power. But even if you're not marrying the future President, images of the couples on these pages are equally motivating... if not more...because these are everyday people who are overcoming everyday struggles with their own expressions of love.

This book is a celebration. If I were a singer I would sing, but my gift is taking pictures. These photos are my love song to you, and I hope it truly sings.

Genuine love exists. It is truly beautiful. It is inspiring. My sincere hope is that this book inspires you to dream, to commit, but most of all...to love.

Ashe'.*

*African and African-American terms noted with an asterisk are defined in the glossary.

In the Beginning...

"In the beginning God created the heaven and the earth. And the Lord God said, It is not good that the man should be alone; I will make him an help meet for him... And brought her unto the man."

Genesis 1: 1; 2:18, 22

DARYL & JANICE

Though neither questioned whether they would ever get married, attorneys Janice and Daryl Maxwell each had their own practical visions of how marriage would be. Understanding that everyone has strengths and faults, Janice envisioned herself, "joining a permanent team with one teammate sometimes giving 70 percent and the other giving 30 percent or vice versa". Daryl was equally pragmatic and optimistic. "People kept telling me, 'when you get married, she'll change'. I never thought that would happen with us…I thought we'd still argue but I thought we both had the types of personalities where things would just resolve themselves."

After three years of marriage (and living together for nearly five) life after the wedding has been much as they expected with few surprises. Both say their biggest shock was how much others would want to be so involved in their marriage--a lesson they quickly learned when the couple agreed that Janice would accept a job out-of-state working on the historic Obama campaign. Janice explains, "When you get married, everyone has their definition of marriage and tries to impose that on you. 'You can't do this, you're married now…You can't do that, you're married now'." Daryl adds that he was just amazed that everyone had such strong opinions about everything from when to have kids to how often they should visit.

"I FELT LIKE SUCH A BAD WIFE. AND I WANTED SO BAD TO BE A GOOD WIFE."

Suddenly there were so many expectations that Janice, normally a high achiever, was feeling like she just wasn't measuring up. It came to a head when one evening, while having dinner with friends, someone strongly suggested that Janice needed to learn to cook for her husband. "I felt like such a bad wife. And I wanted so bad to be a good wife. I was so relieved when he told everyone, 'I knew who I was marrying. I didn't get married to have someone to make dinner for me. I could have gotten a maid for that'."

Later that night when they were alone--Janice still plagued with guilt--couldn't help but ask, "Does it bother you at all that I don't cook like June Cleaver or that we're not like the Cosby's?" Daryl plainly replied, "No. That's not your talent." "I thought it was funny, because I didn't think my cooking was *that* bad, but we laughed and we now use that phrase often when referring to my cooking and other things. I've accepted that they're just not my talents."

"Though we laugh about it now, that's an important conversation to have because not cooking may really bother some men. It just happens not to bother mine."

Daryl agrees on how important it is to have such seemingly mundane conversations, quickly noting one of his own faults. "There aren't many women that could tolerate how much sports I watch" as he reluctantly admits to watching nearly four hours on average each day of sports-related television. Janice has been candid with him about her attempts to understand the importance of "draft day" or watching morning *and* evening Sports Center, but they've found that they're both happier when she can find a good book and leave the sports to him. "Thank God I like to read," Janice chimes in while shaking her head.

Her advice to couples learning to live together is simple. "Know yourself…including your faults. When you can recognize your own failures, it's easier to forgive others' failings. If you see yourself as perfect, then you always want to win…But in marriage, the goal is not to win or be 'right'. The goal is to be fulfilled within your relationship and not take away from the other's fulfillment in that process.

"KNOW YOURSELF…INCLUDING YOUR FAULTS.
WHEN YOU CAN RECOGNIZE YOUR OWN FAILURES, IT'S EASIER TO FORGIVE OTHERS."

And even without a hot, mouth-watering dinner on the table every night ("I can make a mean sandwich" Janice offers), Daryl is clear about why he still feels fulfilled. "I get to spend every day with the person who I wanna tell every story…who I can't wait to tell how boring or how exciting my day was…someone I can't wait to get older and travel with, share the smallest of things together. It's those simple things that I love about being married…and being married to her."

(This page) *Thomas and Kamilah*. Kamilah was very soft-spoken and feminine, and Thomas very masculine. The strength of their individual energies was so traditional, I wanted to give them a traditional Norman Rockwell-like pose--with a twist.

(Opposite page) *Kamilah and Thomas in Love*. Photographed at Malcolm X Park, Washington, DC.

Lori and Sam photographed in Baltimore, MD.

I always give couples the option to shoot engagement photos outside. I think being outside gives shy folks a chance to warm up to the camera a little easier, and emotions tend to be more natural. (Opposite page) *Monica and Mike* (This page) (Top), *Mayra and Brian*. (Left) *Whitney and Paul*.

Al and Sherese. Some couples are naturals in front of the camera and have personalities strong enough for any studio. Al and Sherese came to the studio with lots of excitement and personalized jerseys to match.

Sonia and Jeff. I shot an outgoing Sonia and more-quiet Jeff (right) for a good thirty minutes before Jeff made her tell me she is hearing-impaired. She reads lips that well. Truly an amazing lady, and Jeff, a perfect complement.

EVERY THING BEAUTIFUL...

"He hath made every thing beautiful in his time:
also he hath set the world in their heart, so that no
man can find out the work that God maketh..."

Ecclesiastes 3:11

Robert & Nkenge

"You caught us on a bad day, girl. I hope we can be of some help to you today." Nkenge kindly warns me as she welcomes me into the cozy, immaculately clean town house that she and her new husband of less than one year, Robert, now share.

In the spirit of disclosure, Nkenge admits that they just had a heated discussion earlier in the day, but it doesn't take long for Robert to offer me a drink and both of them to respond to my questions and begin reminiscing about the early stages of their relationship. Nkenge, a youth rehabilitation counselor, and Robert, a motor vehicle operator, got to know each other while working for the same agency. He asked her out a few times and Nkenge finally obliged, but even after their date, Nkenge was not so sure about where the relationship was going. "He was such a nice guy, but he just didn't fit my idea of what I thought my husband would be. Me, in my middle-class 'glory'…I had lists. Mostly, I wanted someone with shared experiences…College, professional experiences, etc." Robert, a hard worker who had once been incarcerated and spent time in the military in lieu of college didn't quite fit her mental picture. "He would joke about my lists like – 'goodness, you won't even give a blue collar brotha a chance!'"

"I gave myself permission to explore him as a person, not as a list of things he could offer--degrees or job titles…"

Little did Robert know that for a large part of her life, Nkenge, 36, had barely given herself a chance. Until she was 28, she carried around pain and insecurity she'd developed in childhood. "I had self esteem issues for a long time. When I was really young, my mom and I moved to a neighborhood where people valued wore what you wore and what you had. And by their standards, with my African name, natural hair and relatively little money, I didn't have much. So I had adopted this terrible mental outlook like, 'if you want to date me, what's wrong with you?'" Even though she had long passed that stage, her unwillingness to articulate that part of her life and non-committal approach to their relationship baffled Robert. "One day she wanted a relationship, the next day, she wasn't sure."

Robert held off pursuing a relationship, but continued to make himself available as a friend. When he volunteered to help take care of her grandmothers' boyfriend and helped her get around after having foot surgery, Nkenge realized that Robert possessed qualities that trumped everything on her list. "He has a heart of gold and he lives his faith every day. Once I saw his heart, I gave myself permission to explore him as a person, not as a list of things he could offer…degrees or job titles." Only then did she accept that they did, in fact, have more in common than she thought--including wanting badly to start a family.

Though he grew up in a single-parent household, Robert, 47, had plenty of time to shape his own ideas of marriage.

"For the first time in my life, I feel like I have a partner."

"While I was in, I had plenty of time to think about what it really meant to be 'free'. And getting married and providing for a family was a big part of that. I really wanted that responsibility." In Nkenge, beyond her veneer, he saw someone with strong morals that shared his passion. "After the second or third date, I knew that she was the type of girl I was going to have to marry. It wasn't going to be any testing the waters." Nkenge laughs when remembering how tightly she held to her religious values of sexual purity until marriage. "He completely respected my morals and I adored him for that. Talk about Christ in action. I had dated men in the church who put up such a holy front, but as soon as they got out of the church, it was like…'okay well we can still do the do'."

Evidently after the wedding, things quickly changed, because Robert and Nkenge are now expecting their first child. Excitedly preparing something every day for their new little one is a welcome and easy change of married life. Other changes are proving slightly more difficult to adapt into daily life. For Robert, the biggest challenge is scaling back and sticking to their mutually agreed financial management plan. For Nkenge, it's normally keeping up with Robert's military-inspired laundry schedule or consistently answering her cell phone.

But each day, they are learning the secrets to a happy marriage, including communication ("even when you don't want to," insists Robert) and being patient with one another. Nkenge sums up, "He's teaching me how to love. I challenge him on a lot of stuff, from eating right to being more focused spiritually…but when I have issues, he really doesn't do that to me. In many ways, he loves me unconditionally, and I'm learning to give that back. It's a beautiful thing. For the first time in my life, I really feel like I have a partner."

Maria calmly awaits the start of a meticulously-planned ceremony. Good planning makes such a difference in brides being able to enjoy the day (and take great pictures).

A bride's wedding day is usually the culmnation of years of dreaming and planning. (Left) This little flower girl could not stop smiling at herself in the mirror (even when others weren't watching). Later, her attention shifts to bridal Barbie and her brand new white patent leather shoes.

I don't believe in "bridezilla". I just assume that every bride wants so badly for their day to match what they've seen and planned in their head for years. They want one day where all of their dreams come true. When it's coming true, there's this smile. I see it on many a face. It's a beautiful thing. (Above) Whitney and Tisha.

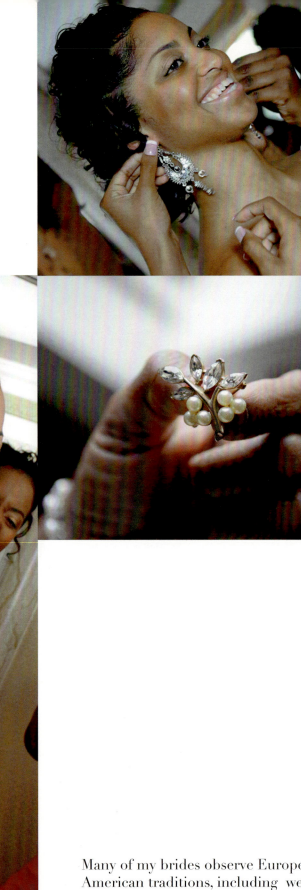

Many of my brides observe European-American traditions, including wearing "something old, something new, something borrowed and something blue". (Left) Joy'El shows off her "something blue". (Right top) Joy'El's girls help her with her jewelry. (Right center) Joy'El's mother holds her mother's broach for me to photograph before it is pinned under her daughter's dress. (The broach actually reminds me of something my own grandmother would have worn).

There are few events that match the pure emotion and excitement of a bride's dressing room. The feminine energy is immeasurable and infectious to women of all ages. (Top) Lori gets dressed in her home for her summer afternoon ceremony. (Above) Lori's aunt and daughter get their first peeks at her in make-up and wedding dress.

(Center above) Bridesmaids try to keep an emotional Zakiya from crying and ruining her make-up. (Left above) A handwritten card from Zakiya's fiancee, Doug, sitting on her beaudoir.

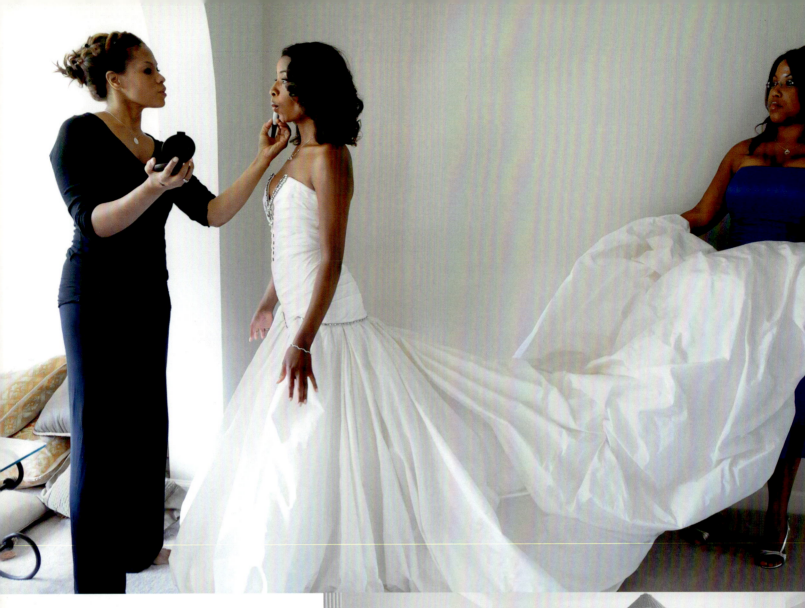

(Above) Loren gets last-minute touches from her cousin who travelled from California to Maryland for the wedding.

(Above) Daphney makes last minute touches to her hairpiece in the dressing room in their villa outside of Nice, France.

(Opposite page) Literally aglow, Tisha stops in the lobby of her hotel before heading to her ceremony.

Minutes before the ceremony are usually the most hectic, but I try to stop brides for at least one portrait before they go down the aisle to get them to calm down and reflect on the moment. I don't tell them to do anything...just look how they feel. These are some portraits I've grabbed before heading out the door. (Clockwise - Caudrean, Loren and Lori).

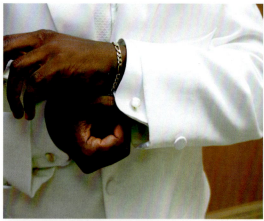

(Clockwise) Sam gets help from his groomsmen (and the internet) as to how to tie a bowtie. (Top) Roy makes sure his cuff links are tight. (Above) James and his groomsmen reflect on their single days. (Left) a trustworthy groomsman shows off the ring.

(Opposite page) (Top) Keith tries hard to focus on putting the final touches on his vows. (Bottom left) A proud Mr. Lucas makes sure his son, Thomas' handkerchief is just right. (Bottom right) Michael addresses final payments for vendors.

(Top) A proud Dr. Wills (back) and his three sons on middle son, Chibale's, wedding day.

(Left) David shares a moment with his son before he walks down the aisle.

(Right) A cool and collected Thomas takes a breather before his stroll down the aisle in Houston.

Grooms tend to be a lot more relaxed. A little alcohol is usually involved (just a little). A lot more energy is focused on being in the right place at the right time.

(This page) (Clockwise) T.C. gets one last spray of cologne from one of his groomsmen. (Top right) Corey and his boys toast before heading into the reception venue. (Above right) Two seemingly unaffected little ring bearers play with action figures while watching guests arrive. (Above left) Mike and his groomsmen share a laugh while posing for formal pics.

(Opposite page) This little ringbearer waits with the "big boys".

Before the ceremony, emotions run the gamut from quiet confidence and well-deserved pride to humility and comic relief. (Above) Kelly and her girls exude timeless elegance.

(Top) Yohance (center) and his boys strike a pose. (Right) Sam and his boys are led in a prayer before the ceremony.

(Below) This whimsical shot nails the emotions of many groomsmen.

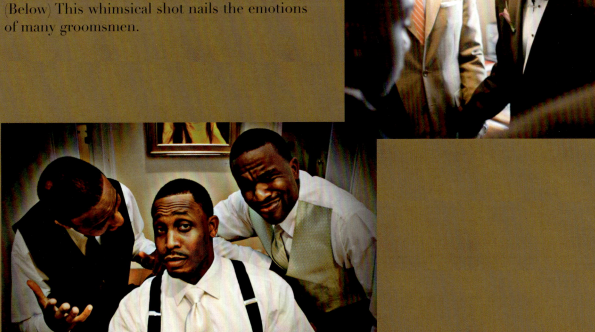

(Opposite and this page) Moments of anticipation immediately before the ceremony.

(Opposite page) (Clockwise) Kristin is squeezed into her tailored dress. (Top right) Maimuna's make-up team adds cowry shells to her hair and finishing touches on her make-up. (Center right) Keida-Ann's bridesmaid can't hide her smile seeing her best friend zipped up into her wedding gown. (Bottom right) Generations of Roux women look on at arriving guests. (Bottom left) Chelai sneaks a peak at the ceremony set-up.

(This page) Monica and her bridesmaids make their way to the church just in time.

(Top left) Keida-Ann gets a kiss from her father before he walks her down the aisle. (Top right) Lisa's mom takes one last look at her daughter before pulling down her veil. (Bottom center) Maria is helped down the stairs.

(Opposite page) Kelley gets her bouquet from her flower girl. (I took a series of portraits of Kelley in this window and couldn't decide which I liked best to put in the book. My other favorite from the series is on the cover).

A SEAL UPON THINE HEART...

"Set me as a seal upon thine heart, as a seal upon
thine arm; for love is strong as death...
Many waters cannot quench love, neither can the
floods drown it..."

Song of Solomon 8:6-7

MIKE & MONICA

After being together for nearly four years, Monica and Mike Barham had come to a crossroads. On top of feeling emotionally drained and unhappy in their jobs, each struggled with their own individual dilemmas at home. Monica suffered terribly from "Catholic guilt" for living together without being married while Mike was overwhelmed by legal issues accumulated during his stint as a pro basketball general manager and wasn't ready to walk down the aisle. Realizing they had hit a wall in their relationship, Monica moved out, purchased a house, and found a new job at a local university. Mike did some soul searching while working through his legal troubles and decided to purue an MBA--embarking on an entirely new career.

It didn't take long for both Monica and Mike to realize that life alone was lonelier than either expected. Mike recalls, "After living together for so long, it was like I had lost my best friend." Monica recalls getting lots of advice from friends telling her to move on, but she just refused to stop believing in Mike. Monica's patience was not in vain. As soon as Mike began to think about marriage, he knew she was the one. "Once I started working towards a future in something I really liked, I felt confident I would be able to provide for my family after graduation. It started to become more clear."

Finally on the same page regarding a wedding, there was just one problem--money. Facing mounting debts, graduate school tuition and a new house note, Monica and Mike put their heads together to devise a plan.

"CINDERELLA WAS DITCHED. IT JUST WASN'T PRACTICAL."

After much debate, they made the tough decision to postpone a traditional wedding and quietly get married in a civil ceremony. "Like most girls, I had grown up watching Disney movies and fairy tales, but real life was shaping up much differently." Monica explains. "Cinderella was ditched. It just wasn't practical. Plus, I didn't want to give him a chance to change his mind!"

After the wedding, Mike took advantage of reduced tuition for staff families at the university where Monica worked. They pocketed the tuition money and began planning an elaborate day to spoil those who had supported them through the years. But even in their wildest dreams they never imagined the profound love that would be showered on them by loved ones -- nor the love that their celebration would rekindle in others. "We got a lot of 'we're inspired' from friends."

Mike, who at times had a strained relationship with his father, was particularly moved by his father's toast to him. "My father and I never got along growing up…to the point where we didn't speak for a long time. But I was amazed how much he remembered about the earliest stages of our relationship. Nothing makes you feel better than having your parents say, 'this is my son/daughter, this is why I'm proud'." The toast gave Mike the opportunity to hear things he never imagined hearing his father say.

Monica remembers most dancing with her own father, who was nearly killed in a truck accident when she was 14. "There was a time when I didn't think my father would ever make it to my wedding. I was so amazingly thankful for that moment."

With such heartfelt moments, guests would have never guessed that the ceremony was not the real thing--until Mike broke the news after the toasts.

"THE MARRIAGE IS VERY MUCH A PART OF THE WHOLE COMMUNITY."

When asked would they advise others to elope, Monica offers, "I would never judge a person's decision to elope, but you owe it to your relationship to do what's best for your relationship. You owe it to those people along the way who helped you become who you are. If you're not prepared to give *that* much to the relationship, I don't know if you are really prepared for this process."

Mike thoughtfully points out the unexpected highlights of their ceremony. "We initially intended the ceremony and reception to be a gift to our family but realized after the fact that being surrounded by everyone was the gift to us. To stand there surrounded by everybody who loves you and to have their energy was just so powerful. Everybody that takes part has a stake. We were made accountable. The marriage is now very much a part of the whole community."

1. Ushers make their way to prepare the aisle for the bride. 2. A wedding officiant lights incense and cleanses the wedding site of unwelcome spirits. 3. With uneven numbers in a wedding party, some lucky guys and gals get two escorts. 4. Baba Caleb offers a gift to his bride's family before taking vows. 5. Flower girls await their turn down the aisle. 6. Little drummer boy. 7. A personalized entry ushers in the bride. (Please excuse the shoutout. One of my clients featured in the book makes these aisle runners--shoutout to Tisha--www.signatureaislerunners.com) I was so happy to get to this wedding and see another bride had purchased one from her.

8.

9.

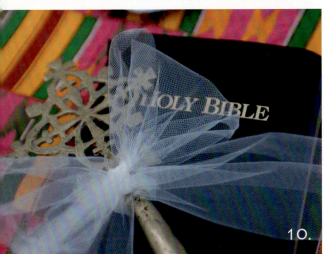

10.

11.

12.

13.

8. Good music makes such a difference in setting the tone of the ceremony. 9. Parents light the candles representing individual families. (I can't tell you how many times the lighter hasn't worked). 10. A stylized Coptic cross and bible resting on a festive kinte cloth represent the seamless melding of African and American cultures. 11. Drummers signal the entrance of bride. 12. A blend of old photos and traditional African sculpture honors family ancestors. 13. A liturgical or modern dance is a favorite addition to a ceremony.

(This page) Brides come up with many creative ways to respectfully include blended family members in the ceremony. Lameka was fortunate enough to have both her stepfather and biological father usher her down the aisle while relatives and guests look on.

(Opposite page) Lameka's fathers give her away.

Expressions on the faces of brides and grooms as they see their spouses come down the aisle. (This page) (Top) Mr. Stith ushers his daughter, Loren to a smiling David (right).

(Opposite page) (Far left) Mr. Lloyd proudly escorts his youngest daughter, Tracy to her groom, Edward. (Top right) A flower girl anxiously grips her bouquet in anticipation of the bride's entrance. (Center right and bottom) Adrian and Corey anxiously wait to see their first glimpse of their new brides.

(Top left) A charismatic Christal is escorted by her father to her waiting groom, Frank (top right). (Above) Nana Yaa is escorted down the aisle by her son, Kwame. (Opposite page) (Right) Corey can't stop smiling at the first sight of his friend and bride, Joy'El. The two had known each other and been friends through undergrad and medical school.

(Previous page) The dusk wedding of Faida and Yohance.

I try to never miss a couples' eyes when they see each other for the first time as man and wife. (Left) Shelley flashes a smile at Kevin when she's pronounced his wife. (Below) Adrian, who normally has a pretty stoic face, lights up when Avril is officially his wife.

(Below) Krystal and Lanell had me, my assistant, and nearly everyone in the room in tears as they recited their vows. Having known each other for 13 years, they had quite a history with one another.

(This page) Lisa and George (Mario). I'd never seen a groom make a bride laugh like Mario did Lisa. (And I loved how he would *watch* her laugh). My shooting partner, Chris, caught these groomsmen that could not keep a straight face.

Officiants have an important role to set the tone and cadence of the event. (Left) A female officiant with a melodic Latin accent set the tone for Mayra and Brian's morning Puerto Rico wedding. (Many thanks to Mayra and Brian for giving me my first opportunity to shoot a Caribbean wedding. They trusted me having seen no samples. God bless them).

(Above) This preacher surprised us all when he interrupted this formal event to deliver a down-home sermon advising everyone in attendance to mind their own business, and "stay out" of the new couples' relationship. (Right center) This minister solemnly gifts a groom a sword, endowing him the responsibility to protect his home at all costs. (Right) Lameka and Kent exchange rings.

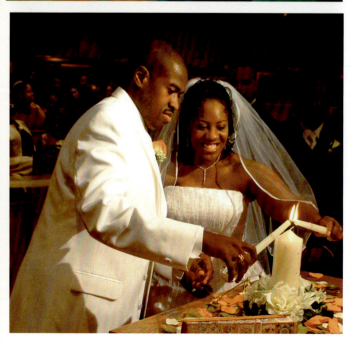

African-Americans have a consummate ability (and right) to accept, adapt and make customs of other cultures our own. (Clockwise) Maasai and Dominique's ocean-side ceremony was officiated by two ministers--one speaking English for the groom's South Carolina relatives and one speaking French, for the bride's family from Haiti. (Top right) Mr. Seevers heads the pouring of libations* for the ancestors. (Above) Joy'El and Corey chose a sand ceremony to symbollize their union. (Left) Crystal and Roy do the same with a unity candle. Faida and Yohance take part in a Yoruba tasting ceremony.*

Weddings don't have to be in an exotic location to be large to be memorable. (Above) Lori and Sam had their butterfly-themed ceremony in the outdoor common area of their townhome development.

(Below) Keida-Ann and Jean scaled down their orignal plans and decided to get married at her uncle's home. Plans for a backyard wedding were even further simplified when storm clouds rolled in and rain started falling 20 minutes before the wedding was to start. Held in the home's family room, their ceremony was one of the most touching I've been blessed to experience. As soon as she came down the aisle of family and friends, the sun reappeared through the windows and all were reminded that God is in control. How divine. (Below right) Keida-Ann's father looks on.

Different images of jumping the broom.* (Top) Lydia and Tim in York, PA. (Center) Paul and Whitney symbolically sweep away the past before jumping. (Bottom) Lori and Sam take the leap.

(Opposite page) Sherese and Al.

Shawnda and Antione exiting their ceremony at historic Metropolitan Baptist Church, a prominent and historic baptist church in Washington, DC.

BETTER THAN WINE...

"Let him kiss me with the kisses of his mouth:
for thy love is better than wine."

Song of Solomon 1:2

JABARI & CHANEL

When Chanel and Jabari Garrett met at a fraternity party in college, the spark was not instantly there. "Jabari was nice, but he wasn't really my type. He was very funny, kind of loud and dressed like all the other guys in my neighborhood…Timbs (Timberland boots), white T-shirt and sweats. I was more quiet, and my mom had told me that men should be nicely dressed…" When asked what exactly was she looking for, her memory gets a little more blurry. "I don't know. I guess I was looking for someone more clean cut, I guess people would say 'pretty'. You know…nice slacks, casual sweater."

"I didn't own a sweater until I was 22," Jabari admits.

"THE THING THAT ATTRACTED ME TO HER WAS ALSO WHAT SCARED ME."

Jabari had a totally different set of reservations. "When I met Chanel, I thought she was pretty, but the thing that attracted me to her was also what scared me. I was an athlete in school, and women always approached me. But it was a chase with Chanel…it was a challenge 'cause she was not as amenable as other women. I was like, 'I'm gonna have to work that hard forever just to keep it up. Unlike other women, Chanel would actually say, 'I need you to do this, to do that to be in my life.' But on the flip side, all men are competitive, and we're attracted to someone when we have to put in work. It makes us feel like we've really accomplished something when we win her."

Evidently, Jabari was up to the challenge because four years later, Chanel is still smiling and their home is filled with the laughter of their 2-yr-old son, Jeremiah. Both admit that they have a very easy going life for the most part, strengthened by their faith in God, nearby family and well-meaning friends. But they also acknowledge that their marriage has not been without its trials, the first of which both admit was caused by a breakdown in communication.

"When something is said that upsets Chanel, she keeps it in. I will say something right then and there. I told Chanel, I can't read minds, but I can read emotions. I definitely know when something's not right, but I cannot pull it out. You have to tell me."

When asked how Chanel dealt with the initial challenge of spilling her guts, Chanel tries to began the difficult conversation by saying, "Look, I'm in this forever, and if we're going to be together forever, I want us to at least be happy. We need to talk."

"EVEN NOW, I HAVE TO REMIND MYSELF THAT I'M A GROWN WOMAN WITH MY OWN FAMILY."

Chanel still finds it difficult at times to express herself when she's not pleased. "I've always been a very quiet people-pleaser. I didn't have pressure from my family to be that way, but there were always high expectations. I never wanted to disappoint anyone. Even now, I have to constantly remind myself that I'm a grown woman with my own family and I can make my own decisions."

"Grown and sexy," chimes Jabari.

When asked what's been the most memorable moment of their four-year marriage, their answers flow readily to the day they got married and other moments they've shared together since.

"When Chanel was saying her vows at the wedding, and she was crying. She's usually not an emotional person, so it was a big surprise that she let herself be so vulnerable in front of all those people."

Chanel also remembers the words from his vows, but remembers more vividly the look on his face when she gave birth to Jeremiah. "To see the joy on his face at that moment…That was a different level of joy."

(Left) *Tracy with Henna**. (Top) *Tracy and Edward* (Wheaton, MD). (Above) *Dominique and Maasai* (Hilton Head, SC).

Adrian and Avril. Both have quiet and somewhat private personalities. Raised with many brothers, Avril was so beautiful, confident and strong. I just love the look in her eyes.

(Opposite page) (Top) *Reginald and Kelly on the Avenue* (Washington, DC). (Bottom) *Thomas and Daneka Stopping Traffic* (Houston, TX).

Paul, Whitney and Friends (Prince George's County, MD). (I wish I had gotten a picture of the bridesmaids' faces when I told them we were going to walk through the corn field in their shoes on this hot, summer day. Fortunately, they were real troopers.)

(Clockwise) *Daphney on the Mediterranean.* (Above and right) *Daphney and Andrew in Old Nice* (Nice, France).

Daphney and Andrew at Place Massena. (Daphney, a school teacher, was as elegant as could be, stopping traffic in downtown Nice. Everyone thought she was a professional model).

James, Takeisha and Friends. (Ocho Rios, Jamaica). A fun and stylish couple, Takeisha and James had a group of their friends fly down to Jamaica and spent the week partying and ending with a beautiful wedding on the beach.

(Left) *Rochelle and Barry.* A fly older couple, they showed me marriage can be just as fun the second time around.

(Below left) *Jamal and Tisha.* Tisha always talked about Jamal and her starting their legacy. I wanted to give them a picture they could be proud to show the grandkids.

(Opposite page) *Jeena and Phillip.* A quiet, but strong young couple, their wedding was only 20 or so guests. I wanted their pictures to be equally quiet and strong.

Rukiya and David. (Thanks to Rukiya for risking the wrath of the venue coordinator by laying across the piano to get this shot).

A TIME TO DANCE...

"To every thing there is a season
and a time to every purpose under the heaven:
A time to be born and a time to die; a time to plant
and a time to pluck up that which has been planted;
A time to weep and a time to laugh;
a time to mourn, and a time to dance."

Ecclesiastes 3:1-4

Kelley & Chelai

After working together for nearly two months on a neighborhood community day planning committee, Kelley Johnson was still unsure whether his co-chair with the nice legs, Chelai, was truly interested in him. What caught his eye even more than her legs was watching her take to task a non-performing vendor, while keeping her class. "She was all business-fied but could handle her own. That turned me on!"

After a meeting one afternoon, Kelley offered to drop Chelai at the bank after one of their meetings on his way home. Ready to pull off and leave, Kelley heard a voice say, "Stop. Stay here. This is where you need to be. This is who you're going to marry." Certain that it was the voice of God, he stayed in the car for over thirty minutes making excuses about how he wasn't ready to get married, he barely knew the girl, but God repeated himself three times.

Chelai came out of the bank, surprised to find Kelley still waiting in the car. "You still here?" she asked, "Yeah, I'm trippin." He never said anything else about it to her until years later.

Their journey from that day to marriage was filled with challenges and higher callings. After three proposals, two years of abstinence, years of graduate school and diligent spiritual seeking…Chelai and Kelley finally both matured to the point in life and in Christ where they both felt comfortable walking down the aisle and pledging their lives to one another.

"The whole submission thing is my biggest challenge."

Both openly admit that even after years of marriage and a beautiful daughter, maintaining a biblically-based marriage remains a challenge. "The whole submission thing is my biggest challenge," admits Chelai. "The first time Kelley exercised his 'authority' was one morning when my girls and I were supposed to go to brunch there was a winter storm passing over our area. My girls were still going and when they called I told them I was on my way. Kelly overheard and was like, 'On your way where? Not in this weather'. I was stunned. I thought he was playing. I came back 20 minutes later ready to go and was like 'Are you serious?' I stayed home, but I really struggled with that."

When asked how she overcame that struggle, she shares: "I prayed and prayed and prayed…and the [snow] storm actually did get really bad…I eventually realized that he was looking out for my safety."

But that wasn't until two days later.

"I had dated other people, but she was always who I would compare them to."

For Kelley, his biggest struggle came before the marriage, when Chelai declared that she wanted to practice abstinence until she was married. "It made me really check myself… 'Am I really gonna marry this person? Am I gonna just wait till she slips up?' I really had to evaluate some things." Kelly openly admits that it was hard and that in his weakest moments, he reflected on others he had dated in the past, but he always respected Chelai. "Most Black women, you could whisper something in their ear and they'd give in, but she was strong and I respected that. I had dated other people but she was always who I would compare them to. I was constantly evaluating…and no one offered what Chelai offered. Who did I have more fun with? Who was broadening my horizons? Who was offering more intellectually and spiritually? Who did I miss most when they weren't around? She was it."

And he adds, "and when we finally did it the right way, it was the best thing ever. Nothing I'd ever done before could compare. It was worth it."

Couples make their entrance to greet family and friends. (Left) Whitney and Paul make a dancing entrance to their reception, which featured a live go-go band.

(Top) Brian gives Anna a little something to work with as they enter their reception.

(Opposite page) (Top) Shawnda and Antione make an entrance at their brunch reception where family and friends have been anxious to greet them. (Bottom right) One family member makes the most of his contribution to the dollar dance*.

(Top and top left) Dancing and drumming celebrate the entrance of Krista and Wayne. (Above and left) Crystal and Omar make a spectacular entrance complete with drummers, dancers and are showered with cash by relatives. (Opposite page) Crystal lives her dream of a *Coming to America* - themed reception (inspired by the 1988 Eddie Murphy film).

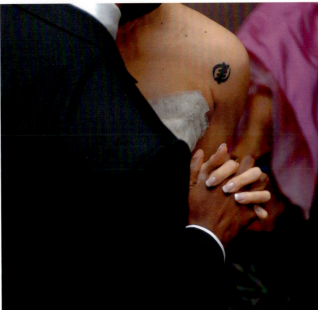

First dances take many shapes and forms. (Above) Little Zuri finds her way into her parents', Tracy and Edward's, first dance. (Above right) Faida and Yohance lock hands for their first dance. (Above center right) Lawrence wipes a tear from an emotional Sharon. (Below right) This little boy and girl begin dancing as a joke to imitate the married couple who had just danced.

(Opposite page) (Top) Chibale and Toni take their first spin on the dance floor as man and wife surrounded by on-looking family and friends. (Bottom far left) Al and Sherese struggle to get their steps together for their upbeat first dance. (Bottom center) Mrs. Ballard, mother of the bride, watches her daughter, Joy'el's first dance. (Bottom right) Jabari serenades Chanel with his best Teddy Pendergrass impression during their first dance.

There's nothing better than a good, heartfelt toast. The more revealing the better. In our culture, this is one of few opportunities to publicly praise and profess our love for one another.

(This page clockwise) (Top left) Mr. Denerville wishes his daughter and new son "a marriage modern enough to survive the times and traditional enough to last forever".

(Top right) Mr. Quansah shares a story of the time he spent a week visiting his son, Phillip who was recovering from surgery. After observing how well his then-girlfriend, Jeena took care of him in his illness, he looked at his son, Phillip and said, "Woupe wie ha wope dien", a Twi saying which translated means, "If you don't want this, what else *could* you want?"

(Below) Keida and Jean, receive toasts from their family at the head of their uncle's dining room table.

(Opposite page) (Top) Mike and Monica publicly reveal to guests, for the first time, that they actually got quietly married in a civil ceremony nearly a year earlier (see p. 51). (Bottom left) Monica shares a dance with her father who almost died in a car accident when she was 14 years old. (Bottom right) Mike absorbs his father's words.

The celebratory spirit of the people New Orleans runs deep, as seen at this New Orleans native's reception (held not long after Hurricane Katrina). (Above) the elder of the family, (Aunt Del) leads the second line. (Left center) Latasha and William dance together in the center while (left bottom) guests pull out their white handkerchiefs to wave the couple on.

(Opposite page) Although all are not pictured, I have great respect for the deeply rooted traditions of each of the Black fraternities and sororities. Black Greek organization ties are often life-long connections passed on through generations. (Top) Faida is serenaded by her husband and his fraternity brothers of Alpha Phi Alpha Fraternity, Inc.. (Bottom left) Shelley receives a tribute from her husbands' fratenity, Kappa Alpha Psi, Fraternity Inc. (Bottom center) The bros of Alpha Phi Alpha Fraternity, Inc. show off their stepping technique. (Bottom right) Chelai is serenaded by sorors of all ages from Alpha Kappa Alpha Sorority, Inc. (Bottom right corner) Magnus' son is instructed in proper hand positioning by members of his dad's fraternity, Kappa Alpha Psi Fraternity, Inc.

Couples add their own twist to long-held European traditions. (Opposite page) (Top) Levin puts on a show before grabbing the garter from Tracey. (Center) Joe gets James Brown treatment for his approach to Lynn's garter. (Right) Mike is surprised by Monica's Pittsburgh Steelers garter. (Below left and center) Corey chooses to retrieve Joy'El's garter with *without* hands. (Bottom right) Craig and Natasha play a practical joke on guests expecting a garter.

(This page) (Top) Though occasionally some women choose not to participate in the ritual, Lydia's girls are pretty indicative of most bouquet tosses where women compete fiercely to catch the prized bouquet. (Bottom left) Men, on the other hand, are normally a different story when the garter is tossed--often stepping away from the tossed garter and sometimes even passing it off (as Van Ness' boys do above).

(Above) Krystal and Lanell are cheered on by members of their bridal party. (Right) There's always one on the dance floor that just goes all out. This little boy is doing his thang.

(Opposite page) (Top left and right) Mario and his boy take it back to the "old school" with the "Snake" and the "Wop", two dances made popular in the 1980's. (Center) Tanisha gets low to the "The Cha-Cha Slide" the lyrics of which challenges dancers, "How low can you go? Can you take it to the floor?" (Bottom left and right) Stephanie and Magnus are egged on to the center of the dance floor by family and friends eagerly cheering, "Go Stephanie! Go Magnus! It's your wedding day! (Cleverly substituting the lyrics to a popular 50 Cent song, which chants, "it's your birthday" with "it's your wedding day").

The Electric Slide* and a Soul Train Line*...Need I say more? (Top left) A bridesmaid breaks out with the robot, a Soul Train line mainstay. (Bottom far left) Mr. Thomas, the groom's grandfather, gets his turn to strut down the line. As the sharpest dressed man at the reception, other guests playfully remove dust from his jacket and sweep his path to make sure he stays "clean". (Bottom center) Ladies do a pretty version of the "Step in the Name of Love" line dance. (Bottom right) David breaks into a mean robot in the French Riviera at Daphney and Andrew's reception at a villa outside of Nice, France. Gotta love it.

(Top) Jabari and Chanel cut their cake before an audience of church family and friends. (Bottom) Chibale and Toni cut their cake and share their first toast with arms intertwined.

(Top) Mrs. Kenner dances with her son, Craig to a gospel song. (Center) When prompted by the DJ to give a kiss to someone you love, this man planted a kiss on his aunt's cheek to thank her for her years of support. Left) Dekisha shares a laugh with her dad. Mr. Posey had raised his daughter as a single dad. I distinctly remember him being the first father to come to the studio helping his daughter plan her big day. After their first dance, he joked that he was just happy to hand her off to her husband, but he was one of the most loving and charismatic fathers I'd met.

AND THEY SHALL BE ONE...

"Therefore shall a man leave his father and mother, and shall cleave unto his wife: and they shall be one flesh."

Genesis 2:24

WAYDE & FELICIA

One of the first things confirmed playboy, Wayde Powell, noticed about his future wife was her walk. "Felicia has a very powerful walk. She's very confident, holds her head up and always looks like she's on her way to do something."

After their first few dates, he understood why. Between earning her Master's degree, traveling and singing opera, Felicia was a busy woman with many things she wanted to accomplish. "I was impressed. I had never had a woman quite on that level," Wayde laughs. "I was like, 'Wow. I gotta step up my game'."

"WHEN YOU'RE RAISED IN A FAMILY OF WOMEN AS I WAS…I WAS TAUGHT THAT IF I GAVE UP SOMETHING, I HAD LOST."

As their relationship grew, the couple found that some of the very things that initially drew him to her were causing the biggest conflicts. "When you're raised in a family of women as I was, you don't see a man and woman working together towards anything in the home. You learn to make decisions and make things happen. I was told not to submit or let anything or anyone keep me from moving forward. I was taught that if I gave up something, I had lost. I had allowed someone else to 'take' something from me."

Felicia's take-care-of-business approach left planning and visionary Wayde baffled and frustrated. Raised in a very traditional home where his father and grandfather worked and the women "cooked and kept the living room clean", when a challenge arose, both he and Felicia would jump to solve it, often butting heads. He found himself explaining to his wife, "I'm a good man. I really do want to take care of my family. I don't want you all to just be out there. I'm here. Let me do what a man's supposed to do."

If Felicia would insist on handling it, a trait she thought was a plus, Wayde would just shut down. "I had to learn that when I wasn't happy with a situation, I couldn't just go off and take control and say, 'I don't like A-B-C'. I had to wait and approach it differently. I had to let him do it his way a few times and say, 'Baby, next time when you do it, instead of doing it this way, why don't you try [whatever]'. It took me a good three years to learn that. As a matter of fact, I'm still working on it" she says with a guilty glance at Wayde.

Wayde has also learned the importance of communicating his plans and respecting Felicia's flow and manner of getting things done (which is far less pragmatic than his). "He plans a week out and those plans are not easily changed. I plan, but it's more like *two* days out…I'm more spontaneous," Felicia points out. Wayde recalls things a bit differently, "Kea, one Sunday we got a call at 3 to be at her family's at 4!" He admits that when they go, he normally has a good time, so he's learned to deal with it, but they both realize how fragile the marriage balancing act can be and what's ultimately at stake. "One of the things that made me love her was all of the things that she does. I don't want to stop her from doing those things. So when I'm making plans, I've got to keep in mind that it's not always about me."

"IT'S HEARTBREAKING BECAUSE THERE ARE BROTHERS OUT THERE…WHO ARE MAKING PLANS…TRYING TO SET UP FOR OUR FAMILY'S FUTURE. BUT IT'S NEVER THAT SIMPLE."

"It's a struggle and at times it's heartbreaking because there are brothers out there that want to do the right thing…not to control…but who are optimistic and making plans. We just need a chance. I'm really trying to set up for our family's future. But it's never that simple…It takes a lot of work."

Now blessed with a busy 2-year old, the couple is planning to purchase their first home. At times, Wayde admits they both get disappointed that things aren't moving as quickly planned, but he's not discouraged. "It will come." And even with all of their struggles, when Felicia walks across a room, she still catches his eye. "I still look at her like, 'Yeah…that's my boo'."

Different endings to the big day. (Above) Geane and Maimuna enlist the aid of their parents to release doves following their wedding reception. (Left) Davone and Patricia finally get a minute to relax in the limo after a long and full day. (I think many couples feel this way after their ceremony and reception. Many people joke about a "hot" wedding night, but most just want a few hours of rest).

(Right) Dominique and Maasai. A simply elegant couple, their entire wedding day on the ocean in Hilton Head, SC was like a dream. It inspired me to give them an equally dreamy and romantic image. (It's been years since, but I still vividly remember Maasai toasting his new wife at their reception saying, "I want to first apologize to my wife...for taking so long to propose. I knew after two months that you were the one.")

IT SHALL BE FOREVER

"I know that whatsoever God doeth, it shall be forever: nothing can be put to it, nor anything taken from it: and God doeth it that men should fear before him. That which hath been is now; and that which is to be hath already been; and God requireth that which is past."

Ecclesiastes 3:14,15

ANTIONE & SHAWNDA

To see them snuggled up on their oversized family room sofa, I would have never guessed there was a time when neither Shawnda nor Antione Howard saw themselves ever getting married. "Oh no," they both echo recalling how they both felt. Between Antione's parents, he had seen six marriages, while Shawnda grew up in a single parent home and watched her own family members languish in unhappy marriages. Convinced marriage wasn't for her, she clearly remembers telling her sister, "I'm never getting married."

Her experience had so shaped her that even after being approached by Antione, a hard-working software developer working a second job as a personal trainer, she was still resistant—refusing to call it a date. Not comfortable with Antione being four years her junior, Shawnda held tight to her reservations. "She was like, 'We can go out, but it won't be a date'." Antione remembers, "I said, 'Okay, we'll call it a get together'." That first "get together" ended up lasting two days with a movie, growing into dinner at Ruby Tuesdays, a game of pool, a few hours of rest (at their own respective apartments) and church the next morning. Antione had such a good time, he went out on Monday, bought some flowers and set them on her doorstep.

Neither had any clue that that "get together" would be the answer to many of their own prayers and those of their families.

"WHAT IS MY PURPOSE, WHAT AM I SUPPOSED TO BE DOING?"

"We were having a great time, talking and hanging out, but when we met I was really trying to grow and mature in Christ. I was in classes and praying trying to get answers to serious questions… 'What is my purpose, what am I supposed to be doing?' People around me were finding their passions and I had a career but was still wondering, 'What is my spiritual gift?'"

The answers came slowly, but in ways that Shawnda never expected. "I realized that one of my purposes was identifying vicious cycles in my family and trying to stop them." A purpose she found that she and Antione both shared. Antione's cycles were somewhat different. "My parents met at Florida A & M, but didn't graduate. I did it for them. Even though my dad had been married many times…when I told him I was engaged, he told me he expected me to 'end the cycle'. My dad would tell me all the time, 'The only thing I regret doing was not staying with your mother'."

Determined to fulfill their purpose, they chose not to live together during their two-year engagement. Instead, they worked together to map out an ambitious plan. After a small wedding ceremony, they sealed the deal as business partners, founding an asset acquisition company, "NexGen LLC" (short for Next Generation) providing a financial foundation for generations to come.

NexGen purchased their first investment property with the profits of the sale of Shawnda's condo when they moved in together and grew quickly, acquiring four properties. But with the downturn of the economy in 2006, NexGen took a hit and Shawnda and Antione had to sell a property and make some serious sacrifices to keep things afloat. "Our toughest challenge has been what everybody's struggling with—the economy. We had to supplement the rent from a couple of the properties for a while and all the eating out, going on spontaneous weekend getaways was over."

That extra time in the house was well spent though and resulted in their now three-year old son, Aaron…whose little life achievements allow Shawnda to see manifest the second part of her revealed purpose. "I think my second purpose is to share knowledge and teach," and Aaron is by far her most prized student. "I am most proud when he tells me, 'Let me do it myself'. I step back and say, 'Okay, we did a good job.' I love to see him gain his independence."

"NOT ALL OF US ARE SUPPOSED TO GET MARRIED…BUT YOU DON'T WANT TO MISS OUT ON YOUR PURPOSE HOLDING ON TO THINGS FROM THE PAST."

Although married life has been good for them, Shawnda and Antione are careful not to push marriage on everyone. Antione offers, "Travel your own path. If your heart's not into it; if you have serious reservations, I mean real serious reservations, you have to decide for yourself. Some people may not have the faith to jump out there." Shawnda agrees, but adds, "Have a conversation with your God…and ask why you are having reservations. Seek what's in His plan…because not all of us are supposed to be married, but we all are supposed to build from experiences we've gone through. You don't want to miss out while holding on to things from the past."

Now expecting their second child, when asked do they ever feel overwhelmed with pressure to correct the mistakes of their families' past, Shawnda replies, "Well it's not really pressure, but there's just …[gosh I'm at a loss for words…] a heightened awareness that it's so much larger than me. It's hard to explain, but …this thing marriage, as I have experienced it… is very important…it's more than important—it's bigger than both of us."

GLOSSARY OF TERMS

Ashe' – Closest translation, "so be it" (similar to "amen"). A word used to speak a thought into being; activating the all-pervasive spiritual energy that animates all creation. Inherently acknowledging the power of word to shape action. Swahili origin. Biblical reference: "In the beginning was the Word" (John 1:1).

Cowry Shell – Decorative snail shell used to symbollize fertility, womanhood, birth and/or wealth. Once used as currency in Ghana, India and China.

Electric Slide – Group line dance created by dancer/choreographer Ric Silver to the song, "Electric Boogie," performed by Marcia Griffith and written by Bunny Wailer, common law-brother of Bob Marley.; created in the 70's and made popular in the 80's.

Henna – Elaborate decorative painting of a woman's body with paste made primarily from henna plant; used in ancient Egypt; widely practiced along the Atlantic coast of Africa, the Middle East and South Asia by primarily Muslim and Hindu faiths; used to celebrate special occasions; tattoo lasts four to six weeks.

Jumping the Broom – African-American custom practiced by enslaved Africans who did not have rights to legally marry. A formal declaration to the community of the formation of a new household, jumping the broom symbolizes sweeping away the past and beginning anew.

Libations – Pouring or drinking of water; acknowledging connection to ancestors; practiced by the Yoruba.

Money Dance - Guests pin money to the bride for a dance or on the couple, wishing them prosperity and offering money for the honeymoon. Origin unknown (commonly practiced at Nigerian, Latin and Slavic weddings).

New Orleans Second Line – Celebratory march fashioned after the "second line" at New Orleans Jazz funerals. Bride and groom normally wave decorative umbrellas and or handkerchiefs serving a dual purpose of guarding from the heat and evil spirits. French-Creole/Haitian origin, practiced by African-Americans in Louisiana.

Ring Shout – African celebratory circular dance formation originally reserved for religious celebrations; secular variations include giving individuals an opportunity to come to the center of the circle; acknowledges individuality and part of a whole; practiced throughout the African diaspora, particularly in Georgia Sea Islands, Jamaica, American South.

Soul Train Line – Secular variation of the ring shout adjusted for better television viewing; made popular by the 1970's Black teen dance show, "Soul Train" hosted by Don Cornelius.

Unity Candle – Candle lighting ceremony representing the union of two families. An elder from both the bride and groom's family lights two individual candles. Then, the bride and groom together light the center candle and blow out the individual family candles leaving only the center candle burning.

Sand Ceremony – Ritual symbolizing the inseparable unity of the married couple. The bride pours sand from one vessel into another while the groom pours from another into the same vessel. A third or fourth person (children) may be added to acknowledge the combining of the family.

Liturgical Dance – Non-secular dance meant to praise the Creator. Biblical reference "Praise him with the timbrel and dance..." Psalm 150:4

Yoruba Tasting Ceremony – Symbolic ritual that includes both members of the couple tasting various foods to represent acceptance of the varying stages of a lifelong marriage. Couples may choose foods to represent each of the elements, but widely used choices are: lemon (sour, harsh words), vinegar (bitter), cayenne (hot, spicy, sexy) and honey (sweet, comforting and joyous). Water is sipped between tastings to symbolize moving forward. Also referred to as the "Tasting of Four Temperments."

SYMBOLS USED IN THIS BOOK

Adinkra symbols were first used by the Akan people of West Africa to easily communicate cultural morals, values and beliefs. Each symbol has layered meanings.

**Onyankopon adom
Nti biribiara beye yie**
"By God's grace, all will be well."
Symbol of hope, providence and faith

Me Ware Wo
"I shall marry you."
Symbol of perseverance and commitment

Akoma
"The heart"
Symbol of patience and tolerance

Nyame Nti
"By God's grace"
Symbol of faith and trust in God
Stalk symbolizes that food is a basis of life and that survival would not be possible if not for the food that God has placed on Earth for nourishment.

SOURCES

CameroonStar. "Nigerian American Wedding Reception Native Nigerian Dance." (posted May 7, 2009) http://www.youtube.com/watch?v=fPpYl4L5PCg (accessed January 21, 2010)

Cole, Harriette. Jumping the Broom, Second Edition: The African-American Wedding Planner. New York, NY: Henry Holt and Company, LLC; 2004.

The Knot contributors, "Ceremony: 7 Afrocentric Wedding Traditions", The Knot, http://wedding.theknot.com/real-weddings/african-american-weddings/articles/7-afrocentric-wedding-ceremony-traditions.aspx (accessed January 23, 2010).

Oracle Band contributors, "Electric Boogie – Marcia Griffiths (AKA "Electric Slide") Song Information/Chart History/Lyrics", http://www.oracleband.net/Lyrics/electric_boogie.htm (accessed December 30, 2010)

Poniewaz, Carrie May. "The History of Henna Tattoo Design" Pagewise
 (2002) http://www.essortment.com/all/historyofhenna_rmfe.htm (accessed January 20, 2010)

Rahman, Juell. "History of the Henna Tattoo." History of the Henna Tattoo EzineArticles.com. http://ezinearticles.com/?History-of-the-Henna-Tattoo&id=1760632 (accessed January 21, 2010)

Walker, George. "The New Orleans Second Line Parade." Associated Content, http://www.associatedcontent.com/article/2153891/the_new_orleans_second_line_parade.html?cat=16 (accessed January 23, 2010).

Wikipedia contributors, "Bunny Wailer," Wikipedia, The Free Encyclopedia, http://en.wikipedia.org/w/index.php?title=Bunny_Wailer&oldid=335900352 (accessed January 23, 2010).

Wikipedia contributors, "Cowry," Wikipedia, The Free Encyclopedia, http://en.wikipedia.org/w/index.php?title=Cowry&oldid=322616261 (accessed January 23, 2010).

Wikipedia contributors, "Libation," Wikipedia, The Free Encyclopedia, http://en.wikipedia.org/w/index.php?title=Libation&oldid=335673006 (accessed January 23, 2010)

Wikipedia contributors, "Money Dance," Wikipedia, The Free Encyclopedia, http://en.wikipedia.org/w/index.php?title=Money_dance&oldid=318369806 (accessed January 23, 2010).

Willis, W. Bruce. The Adinkra Dictionary: A Visual Primer on the Language of Adinkra. Washington, DC. The Pyramid Complex, 1998.

DECORATION IDEAS...

Don't forget. To be African is to be creative and a true original. Never be afraid to add your *own* personal touch to your special day. But if you need some help getting started, here are a few ideas. 1. Incorporate natural fibers and themes into invitations. 2. Create a ring pillow that respects the environment. 3. Consider simply elegant bridesmaids bouquets by African-American florists. 4. Personalize souvenir programs with hand-tied, earth-hued ribbon or stickers. 5. Give plants as take-away gifts and ask guests to say a prayer for you each time they water it. 6. Light a candle for the missed ancestors at each table. 7. Give a nod to our southern past and create a casual mood with wild flowers and mason jars. 8. Have guests take a Polaroid and leave a personal message in place of a sign-in book. 9. Serve soul food with a twist (fried chicken, sweet potatoes and green beans). 10. Adorn yourself with African-inspired ivory-beaded jewelry or line bouquet with cowry shells.* 11. Combine flower girl and ring bearer in one and having a flower girl hide rings in her bouquet. 12. Decorate shoes with cowry shells. 13. Honor ancestors with a table of their own. 14. and 15. Make cake cutting even sweeter by decorating with African symbols, shells and beads. 16. Include a sweet fruit dessert bar for those with high "sugar". 17. Decorate simple candles imprinted with Akan symbols. 18. Adorn natural hair with orchids.

19. Set a relaxing mood with Caribbean-themed gift bags for visitors from out of town. 20 , 21. Make guests feel special with hand-made place cards. 22. Add Jamaican-brand beverages to give a nod to diasporic heritage. 23. Take some time on the beach and gather shells to provide a natural touch to an ocean-themed wedding. 24. Create a custom cocktail for guests. 25. Show your creativity withh hand-made table cards. 26. Become instant classic in an old classic car. Have the chauffeur play "old school" soul songs. 27. Order a plain cake and decorate with flowers from the bouquet. 28. Rent a photo booth and give guests personalized take-home gifts. 29. Give guests natural mints to inspire romance. 30. Dress up any outdoor space with blossoms. 31. Surprise guests with red velvet or black cake 32. Fill coconut shells with sand and plants to decorate table. 33. Personalize Hershey kisses decorated with photo stickers. 34. Offer hand-made cookies with a heart-warming motif. 35. Switch it up and offer hand-decorated cupcakes in non-traditional flavors.

FINAL THOUGHTS

Wow. Where to begin?

By the way, that's me on the right there in the middle of Latonya and William's wedding.

First of all, thank You God for allowing me to see the things that I see and allowing me to make a living capturing what I see. Thank you for providing for me while I took the time out to put this book together. Thank you for the vision. Thank you for always providing. I pray that You are pleased.

Thank you to my family and friends, who have been tremendously supportive of me throughout my career but particularly for this project. Thanks to my husband, Rob for having my back--always. Thanks for always shoveling the snow. My stepsons Mike, Rob and Rell, my little authors...thank you for bringing such joy to my life. To my parents, you are the best parents anyone could ask for. Thank you for the sacrifices you have made, and continue to make so that I can be successful. The Jackson, Prather and Taylor families--your love has made me who I am and I will always love you for it. Thank you for the legacy you've left me. To my girls from high school and college (Keisha, Erika, Nena, Tai, Tasha, Terri, Gala, Gena, Brina, Shana, Sonia): I love ya'll. I'm so proud you are my friends.

This book would not be possible without the smart, talented and hard-working individual photographers who make up the Imagine Photography team. I am blessed to be surrounded by people who share my passion for photography and have dedicated their lives to becoming the best photographers they can be. Some of the photos in this book are theirs (please see additional credits), but just having them present gives me the freedom to focus on what I do. Chris Thomas, Tulga Dorjgotov and Annie Flanagan--it has been a honor to shoot with each of you. Thank you for putting up with me. To my younger brother and studio manager, Sam...you are so naturally talented and blessed. I've learned much from you. Thanks for bringing Sabrina and Naomi into my world. And to my extended photography family, Chris, Lateef, Jessie, Jane, Earl, Brandy, Quentin, Derrell, Victoria and Dave--thanks for helping me out and always being there whenever I need you.

I am immensely grateful to those countless working photographers who dedicated their lives to documenting the valuable lives of Black people in this country...Gordon Parks, Addison Scurlock, James VanDerZee, Carrie Mae Weems, the many photographers of *Songs of My People*, *I Dream a World* (Brian Lanker) and *Crowns* (Michael Cunningham). Thank you for modeling what it means to capture Black culture with elegance and dignity.

Another debt of gratitude is owed to those who have been particularly supportive of my work and this particular effort. Rondolyn, thank you for support and advice. I couldn't have done this without you! Thanks to the spirit of my aunt Joyce Prather for continuing to inspire me to be an "artist" first. Also thanks to Edith, who took her valuable time to proofread and my mom for proofreading and interviewing those that I could not.

A special thank you to all of my clients--many of whom are pictured in this book, *most* of whom are not. Thank you for trusting me over and over to capture the most memorable moments of your lives. You all have blessed me more than you will ever know. Since I was a child, I dreamed of being a photographer. You make my dreams come true.

Very special thanks to the couples featured in this book. Thank you for allowing me to be in the mix on your special days. Thank you for sharing your stories.

Jabari and Chanel	Max and Beverly	Geane and Maimuna	Joe and Lynn
Jamal and Tisha	Daryl and Janice	Jean and Keida-Ann	Levin and Tracey
Kelley and Chelai	Caleb and Yaa	George and Lisa	Davone and Patricia
Edward and Tracy	Charles and Olusade	David and Rukiya	Craig and Natasha
Maasai and Dominique	Robert and Nkenge	Tim and Lydia	Wayde and Felicia
Brian and Anna	Thomas and Kamilah	Kevin and Shelley	Mike and Tiffany
Keith and Maria	Sam and Lori	Magnus and Stephanie	Andrew and Daphney
David and Loren	Al and Sherese	Kent and Lameka	VanNess and Robin
Barry and Rochelle	Jeff and Sonia	Adrian and Avril	Reggie and Chaunta
Paul and Whitney	Babatunde and Lateicia	Antoine and Shawnda	Brian and Anna
Mike and Monica	Corey and Joy'El	Omar and Crystal	Anthony and Lydia
Yohance and Faida	Derek and Caudrean	Frank and Christal	James and Nyel
Lanell and Krystal	Roy and Crystal	James and Takeisha	David and Tenisha
Reginald and Kelley	Thomas and Daneka	Phillip and Jeena	John and Denise
Nickia and Kristin	Doug and Zakiya	William and LaTonya	Darnell and Dekisha
Brian and Mayra	Chibale and Toni	Wayne and Krista	
	TC and Dionne	Lawrence and Sharon	

I know many of you are probably curious about where each of the couples are now and what's going on with their lives. I also know there are those who will want to delve deeper into what percentage of couples is still married (all but one at the time of printing), who's not represented, the dynamics of socio-economic status and everything else. I seriously debated about whether or not to get into all of that, but quickly realized, that it would be a whole 'nother book! Besides, I have spent many hours painfully listening to discussions about the state of Black relationships and frankly, my heart breaks at the thought of another negative conversation ending in blaming Black men, White men or Black women being blamed.

I wrote this book because the images in this book are what we are dying to see: a vision of how beautiful resolution can be.

Having said that, I offer my most sincere thanks to the couples that agreed to be interviewed for this book and were so honest in sharing your challenges. In our culture, we often celebrate people whose lives really don't warrant such adulation. You all are *real* superstars and your light will shine. Thank you.

Lastly, thank you for reading and buying the book. You will never know how many people looked at me like I was silly for wanting to publish a book of "other people's wedding pictures". But this book was not for them. It was for you. And for the generations to come...so they will know that even in this day and time we, too, were a beautiful people who celebrated things like commitment and family and believed in love.

Even if no one else thinks it's important to remember--I still do.

PHOTO CREDITS

All photos copyright 2009, Imagine Photography.

Photos by Kea Taylor for Imagine Photography unless listed below. Photos by Tulga Dorjgotov, Annie Flanagan and Chris Thomas taken for Imagine Photography.

Page ii (top right, groomsmen laughing - C. Thomas) p.32 (top left-A. Flanagan, bottom left -C. Thomas), p.33 (bottom right - T. Dorjgotov), p.34 (bottom left - C. Thomas), p.36 (top left - C. Thomas. top right - T. Dorjgotov), p.37 (T. Dorjgotov), p.39 (top and bottom - T. Dorjgotov, center - A. Flanagan), p. 59 (bottom right - C. Thomas), p.65 (bottom - A. Flanagan), p. 66-67 C. Thomas), p.95 (top right - C. Thomas), p.99 (top and bottom center - C. Thomas), p.100 (top center - C. Thomas) p. 122 (photo 34 - T. Dorjgotov).

Design note: Historic photos on cover and title page courtesy of Cynthia Prather (authors' parents and grandparents' wedding day photos). Photographer unknown. Gold design from authors' parents' wedding album.

STAY IN TOUCH...

We would love to hear your feedback. Let us know what you think by dropping us an email at:
kea@istilldoweddings.com

To order gift copies of "I Still Do", please visit:
www.istilldoweddings.com

To order limited edition items featuring photos featured in this book, please visit:
www.imaginephoto.printroom.com/istilldophotos

And yes...we still do shoot weddings. To arrange for Imagine Photography to photograph your wedding, reunion or special event, please visit: www.imaginephotographyonline.com
or call (202) 726-0287.